How to Stay Sane in a Crazy World

How to Stay Sane in a Crazy World

A MODERN BOOK OF HOURS TO SOOTHE THE SOUL

SOPHIA STUART

FOUNDER OF teamgloria.com

HAY HOUSE, INC.

Carlsbad, California ▪ New York City
London ▪ Sydney ▪ Johannesburg
Vancouver ▪ Hong Kong ▪ New Delhi

Published and distributed in the United States by: Hay House, Inc.: www.hayhouse .com® • *Published and distributed in Australia by:* Hay House Australia Pty. Ltd.: www .hayhouse.com.au • *Published and distributed in the United Kingdom by:* Hay House UK, Ltd.: www.hayhouse.co.uk • *Published and distributed in the Republic of South Africa by:* Hay House SA (Pty), Ltd.: www.hayhouse.co.za • *Distributed in Canada by:* Raincoast: www.raincoast.com • *Published in India by:* Hay House Publishers India: www.hayhouse.co.in

Cover design: Amy Rose Grigoriou
Interior design: Tricia Breidenthal
Interior photos: Sophia Stuart for teamgloria, inc.

Library of Congress Cataloging-in-Publication Data

Stuart, Sophia.
  How to stay sane in a crazy world : a modern book of hours to soothe the soul / Sophia Stuart, founder of teamgloria.com. -- 1st edition.
    pages cm
  ISBN 978-1-4019-4410-0 (hardcover : alk. paper) 1. Health--Anecdotes. 2. Mind and body--Popular works. 3. Health, Self care. I. Title.
  RA776.5S84 2014
  613--dc23
                          2013033277

Hardcover ISBN: 978-1-4019-4410-0

17 16 15 14   4 3 2 1
1st edition, February 2014

Printed in the United States of America

CELIA

She'd shown me that it was possible to dream big and live large.
She'd moved to New York and now traveled everywhere
in a glamorous job in the world of high finance.

"My darling, I've just gotten back from being around the world,"
I heard her say without preliminaries. "Twice, actually," she added
while I was still wondering what had possessed me to pick up the
phone. It had rung without any reaction on my part. I had ignored
it, I could only assume, for as long as was humanly possible.

"I'm dying to hear the news," she continued.
"How are you? Tell me everything."

Friends of *teamgloria!*

.......................a delicious thank you.

jacqueline, lala, noel, kate, william, barry, george, andrew, james, maria, alexia, debb, olga, tina, bruni, jeannette, jonathan, onestopnyc, john, chris, gym, greg, zippy, jake, rosie, stephen, DE, amy, jason, underpup, jane, d wolf, lotten, heather, jen, stacy, eleanor, greg d, guild, ilicco, kate, jules, uwa, james, matt, ali, javier, habilleuse, jacqueline, cindy, christina, jay, chris, belinda, kristen, lucia, anne, cosine three, kenny, ian, rae, kevin, joseph, nick, cyril, margot, mary, amanda, jw/1, jw/2, ian, lala, larry, anne, sarah, my parents, my brother, my niece, my doctors daniel and chris and dena, carol, olga, my attorney walker, and my friend and agent lisa gallagher.

and most especially to gloria nimbus—wherever you came from—and I'm so grateful you did . . .

CONTEN

INTRODU

CTION

I used to make my living from writing.

And then the newspaper I worked for in England laid off many of its staff, and publications everywhere were downsizing. So I went and tried something else, which required a whole new look from Brooks Brothers. The suit wasn't really me, but it was necessary. I'm sure you know how it is. A decade later (still working as a suit), I started to write again—during nights and weekends and frustrated lunchtimes and long-haul business travel. One of the things I wrote (or which came to me, as I do believe in the whole muse concept) was a screenplay about a character called Gloria, a trainee angel who sat "up there" waiting for her first assignment.

To occupy the hours she ought to have been studying humans and their foibles, Gloria was glued to the new celestial movies-on-demand channel and became obsessed with Doris Day. So you can imagine the confusion that unfolded when she got her first assignment and arrived in modern-day Manhattan. But Gloria, with a carefree joy and bubbling happy attitude, was determined to see the world through rose-colored glasses. So magical adventures started to happen. I loved writing this screenplay about Gloria, and the character's infectious joy started to blossom in my own life.

I was really stressed with my (pretty big) day job, so it helped to look at the world through Gloria's beautiful lens. Otherwise, I was going to crack up. Despite a long career in digital media, it had not occurred to me to write a blog, and my job made it awkward to do so under my own name. Hence the need for writing as Gloria. That blog became teamgloria.com—and I began to document "glorious people, places, and things." As I opened my eyes to the gloriousness around me, the daily trials and tribulations of everyday life eased at last.

But then something terrible happened. My doctor found a tumor in my throat. After a year of regular ultrasounds and biopsies, there were three tumors forming a mass that it took a five-and-a-half-hour surgery to remove. My blog became a place to tell the truth about entering the realm of the unwell. I had no idea how precious and moving it would be to see people responding, linking to me, sharing my words, and adding their own "glorious people, places, and things." They gave me strength through the frightening and painful experience of surgery and recovery.

It was an incredible experience. I became part of a larger online community for the first time—and started to make this book while on medical leave of absence, sorting through all the photographs I had taken while traveling the world for my day job.

During the Middle Ages women of noble birth would have a book of hours, a devotional object that gave them room to pause, to take a moment, to become spiritually refreshed. While convalescing, I thought that perhaps a modern book of hours was needed: some beautiful images and a few carefully chosen words to inspire and soothe a troubled soul. It's a crazy world out there, and most of us are stressed beyond belief.

I decided to keep the book simple, just three sections—morning, afternoon, evening—and have the framework be simple as well: inspiration, perspiration, exhalation. The book is designed to take you through your day in a beautiful, healing, kind way. Each idea and suggestion is accompanied by one of my original photographs from my business travels or a still life from when I was confined to my apartment on medical leave.

Inspiration speaks for itself. This first section is the morning dreamtime, the oh-my-God-wouldn't-it-be-great-if hopes for the future. I offer you some of my photographs from around the world to give you a space for your soul to fly.

Next, you arrive at the afternoon. Feels like hard work to be as inspired? That's why I called it perspiration. Yes. That's the bit when you're at the office, or working at home, or in the world being busy. Through the past twenty (gulp) years of my career, I've picked up tricks and ideas to get me through the business travel, long hours at my desk, office politics, and the sheer uncertainty of the marketplace. And don't forget this is a work in progress (like life itself, right?), so do go online to teamgloria.com and add your own coping tools and send me a picture of how you've made your desk a place of sanctuary!

Then it's the evening time; let's e x h a l e. When I got my diagnosis, I knew that I needed to change my life. This section is called exhalation because it's all about taking a breath, learning how to unwind, to leave the day behind. After my surgery, I had to take a month off work to recover. I had not taken a month off in a decade. It was a shock. And I learned a great deal about exhaling during that period.

Please take the time to look after yourself. Find the gloriousness in your everyday life. Relish the delightful sparks of inspirational magic. You are important. You matter. It took writing as Gloria to help me realize this.

Please don't wait until you get sick, like I did . . .

And don't forget to come and visit us all at teamgloria.com—it would be so delicious to meet you!

MORNING
Inspiration

Dream about far-off **lands.**

Take time to **play.**

Get a new **perspective.**

6

Read a naughty **novel.**

Have **crushes.**

11

Catch a **train.**

Step into the **past.**

Engage your **spirit.**

Visit the **future.**

19

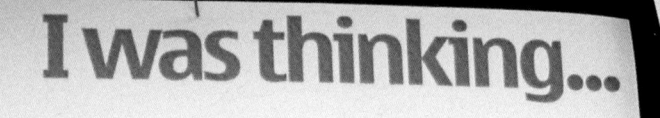

I was thinking...

I NEED TO

SLEEP!

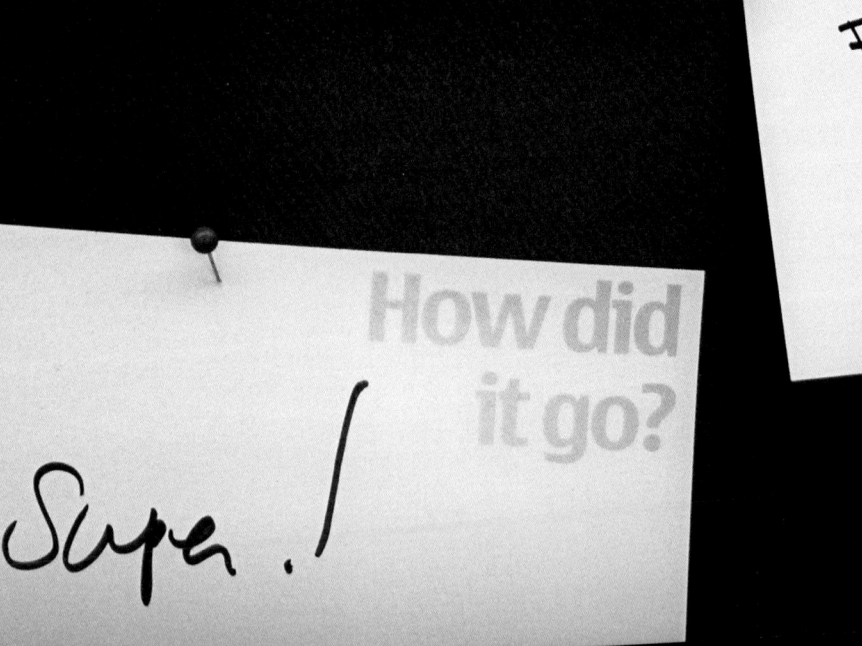

How did
it go?

Supe./

Tell your friends how you **feel.**

Take a walk at **dusk.**

Make a road-trip **playlist.**

Find a place to **write.**

Watch foreign **films.**

Get sand between your **toes.**

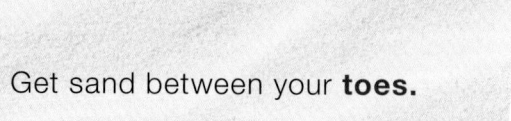

Post a **love letter.**

Swim in cool waters.

Eat raw veggies while **reading** glossy magazines.

Ride a bicycle through **Paris.**

Light candles.

Stand and **admire.**

Call a friend.

Be silent at **sunset.**

Stand up and be **counted.**

AFTERNOON
Perspiration

This is not easy to do.

I know.

But there are various tricks and tips I've learned over the years.

Tip #1: Office (or Cube) Décor. Surround yourself with beauty and things that make you giggle. Suggestions = silly cartoons, geeky toys (I had Asterix the Gaul, C-3PO, and Yoda on a shelf at eye level), achingly glamorous fashion shots from the 1930s (simple white frames from Pottery Barn make vintage magazine pages look like works of art), and interior porn (no, not real porn, unless you work in a Very Liberal Environment)—you know—shots of unbelievably stunning houses and gardens and blue-blue swimming pools in Beverly Hills that make you think "OMG, that's my dream place, and that's why I'm working late again, so help me, God, and my eyes are scratchy, and I want to go home . . . to THAT house, one day."

Tip #2: Lunch. Take It. Every Day. Stop eating at your desk. Tupperware is your friend. Goat cheese, mission figs, a seven-grain roll, and a peach—pack your lunch and go to the park. If you separate the day into halves with lunch, it goes more quickly, and you'll be a nicer person for the second bit. Hey, take a friend. Take two. Have a picnic. Try it.

Tip #3: Fresh T-Shirts. I kept a stack of fresh T-shirts in my middle drawer and changed after lunch. Just felt better. I also had a full set of lady supplies in my top drawer. Not just tampons and makeup remover and basics for retouching of makeup (requirements for tears in the office) and deodorant, but also a needle and thread, spare socks (or panty hose if you're still doing skirts), a toothbrush and toothpaste.

Oh, yes, and after the first fire drill, a battery-powered flashlight.

Tip #4: Hand Cream. I had several different types of hand cream (some were gifts; some I'd bought) on my desk and offered a little dollop to people when they came for meetings.

It's a nice, fragrantly soothing kind of a way to start a work session. Yes, even the men. In fact, I had a not-too-scented and definitely not girly-fragranced one just for the chaps.

Tip #5: Secret Sisterhood. I built a network of women to talk to at work by pretending one already existed. I started to invite other 30-something and 40-something women to tea, one by one, and hinted that there was a secret sisterhood where we all called each other when we needed to vent in safety. Every woman was intrigued and wanted to be part of it. The thing was, I made the whole concept up. But by the time I'd had lots of "teas" in my office, it existed. You need a sisterhood at work. But be careful. Don't get into trouble by gossiping. I used the network to vent without details. Try it. You get to call and say, "Can I just talk for a second? I don't need advice. I'm keeping all the names out of it. I just need someone to listen."

Tip #6: Book Medical Appointments in January. Schedule everything for the year in one go—dental, mammogram, whatever you need. And then don't reschedule like a crazy person. Have all your checkups—you are important. It was at an annual physical that my first tumor was found. And I had almost canceled the appointment because I had a report to do. I shudder to think what might have happened if the tumors had spread undetected. So look after yourself.

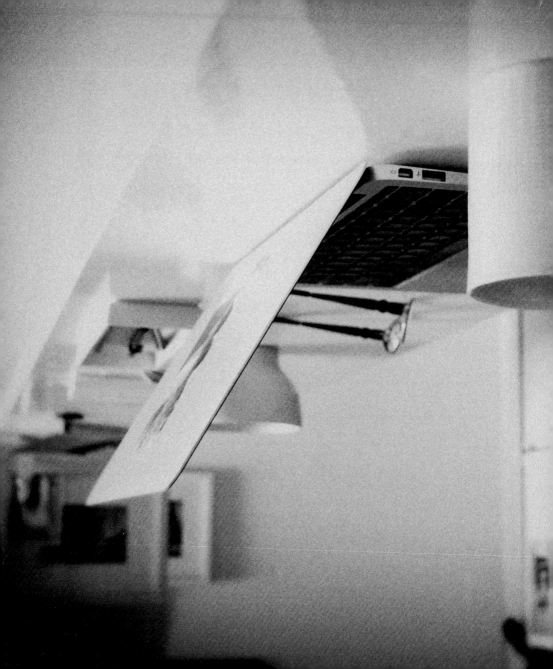

Tip #7: Have a Life. Schedule fun. Have hobbies. Take classes. Make time to see friends. Put it all in your diary (digital or otherwise). Don't let a week go by without having dinner with a friend, seeing a movie, going to bed early one night (with or without chocolate) to read a novel for several delicious hours, downloading a podcast of your favorite author doing a reading and lying on the couch just listening, smiling, and maybe having a little cry.

Tip #8: Answer Two Questions. Every time I saw a co-worker by the coffee/tea/hot chocolate/strange soda machine at the office who looked tired and frazzled, I'd say, "Answer two questions: when is your next massage, and when is your next vacation?" Sometimes people would look annoyed. Hey, their problem, not mine. If you stopped me by the coffee machine, I could always tell you—Tuesday and Los Angeles in February. You need to plan things that make you feel good. And those who never had a massage booked or a holiday planned? I gave them a wide berth after a while. Martyrdom is so unattractive.

Tip #9: Let's Get Physical. Yup, exercise. It works. Trust me. My life changed (and everyone else looked a lot less nervous around me) when I started swimming every other day. It wasn't all about the weight (okay, I'm lying); it was about moving my body and releasing the anger and frustration of the day. If swimming isn't your thing and you don't feel like becoming a yoga type, then get an old-fashioned bicycle (and a helmet, please).

Tip #10: Have a Vision. What's your dream? Maybe you work so you can travel afar. That's great! Then have a folder with clippings of places you'd like to go next. Display framed pictures of your creative work on your desk. Celebrate who you are in Real Life. It's not their job (the Corporation) to "get you." They employ you to be productive, and in return, they pay you. The other stuff— your dreams—is for you to make come true.

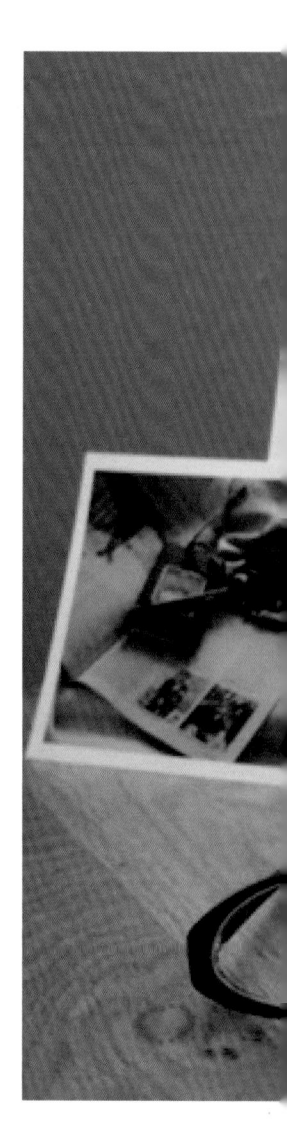

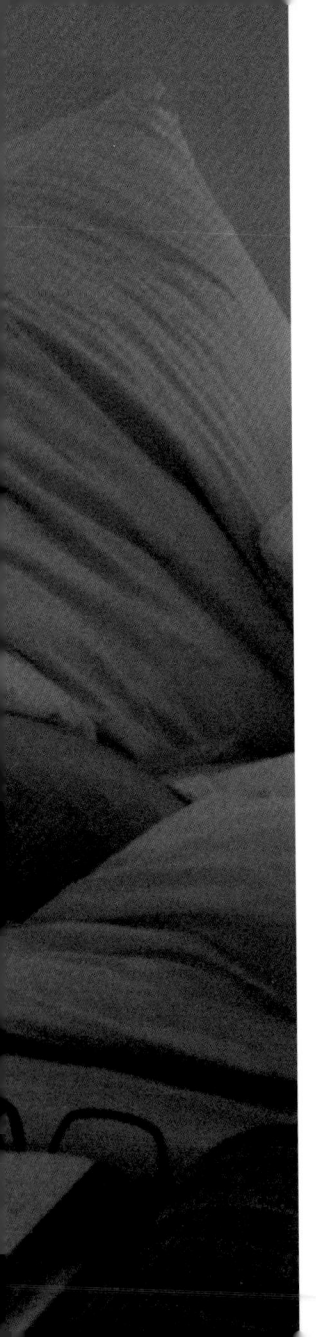

EVENING

Exhalation

HAVE YOU REACHED BURNOUT?

Or has it just been one of those days? Or months? Or years? I was once in a yoga class (a rare yoga class, I'll admit), where the teacher had us all exhale again and again and again, until—as she put it—we'd let go of today, the last month and, by the end, "the whole of last year." We all collapsed in very non-yogic giggling. But we knew what she meant. Exhale. Let it all go.

To exhale, I stop "doing life" and start to wind down and engage in soothing rituals like lighting a candle.

And then I take to my bed.

Perhaps you need to do the same?

Life can be tough and exhausting. Do you know how to rest?

That's what this section is about. Stopping. Exhaling. Rejuvenating. Perhaps not for an entire month of medical leave, which is what happened to me following my surgery.

But if you don't stop and exhale and look after yourself, you, too, might one day find yourself wearing one of those hideous paper gowns with the ties at the back and lying on a gurney wondering how the hell it got this bad. Just saying. ;-)

The world is going to have to do without you.

Just for a while. But it will cope.

Funny enough, that was the hardest thing for me to understand. That my body had broken down, and it would get worse if I didn't take this whole "medical leave" seriously. And the world would do okay without me. Huh? ;-)

There was never a conclusive reason for the appearance of the three tumors (which I nicknamed "Tobias and his sisters"—yes, the Woody Allen reference helped). So I chose to see it as a big lesson. Because, in my experience, either you get the lesson the first time—or it just keeps coming, in different forms and guises, until you do.

So let the world turn without you.

It's your time to leave it all behind for as long as you need, whether that's a medical leave like mine, a week-end of luscious laziness and recuperation, or perhaps a stolen Sunday afternoon.

Ready? Let's do this together.

THE VIEW FROM THE TOP

From 2009 to 2012, this was the view from my office in midtown Manhattan. Yup, it's an impressive sight. But it also deceived me into thinking, and feeling, that I was invincible. (I sort of get the idea that it's meant to.) But the tumors reminded me that I am not.

The first feeling (as we're going to talk about feelings now—bear with me if you come from a part of the world where that is just not done) was UTTER RAGE.

But I didn't know that's what it was. It felt like a cavernous, black, seething hot pit in my stomach. To be honest, it took at least a year for me to calm down after the moment in my surgeon's office when he said, "We found a mass." He said it with sadness, because he's a surgeon and has said that line over and over again to type-A female executives in New York.

And I said, "I've seen this movie and didn't like it."

I had become a statistic, and that made me furious.

Can you relate?

You know how we think we're invincible and then—*wham*—something comes along that we can't control? That's how it felt.

If you're feeling that now, for whatever reason—illness, stress, breakup, post-rehab, last trimester and can't move—hang in there.

To get a view like this, you have to fight your way to the top. The tumors proved to me the fight had not been worth it. It had broken me. Don't get me wrong; the lady-executive life had its moments (and don't cry for me—a lot of those moments happened on far-flung business trips to places I'd always wanted to see, like India, and while staying in luxury in five-star hotels in Paris, Milan, and Beijing), but boy, was it exhausting.

Thank God for the health insurance.

DO YOU FEEL ANGRY THAT YOU'RE SICK—
OR STRESSED—OR JUST BEYOND TIRED?

Good.

Feelings are a useful barometer. At least I found them to be so—despite the fact that, for me (you too?), they are often a delayed reaction.

What do you do with your rage?

I wrote. A lot. Most of it on my blog, *teamgloria* (teamgloria.com), some of it in my blank notebooks, and a great deal of it in e-mail or on old-fashioned pen and paper and pretty cards sent by post. The funny thing about writing is I can't lie to myself when the pen hits the page. You probably haven't written on a regular basis since those heartfelt teen diary entries, right?

I also went to the local cinema that has a mini arcade and played the hell out of Time Crisis. It's one of those old-school video arcade games with a screen and everything, and it really helped to blow up a few things. As did all the movies I watched.

And taking long, hot baths.

For me, there's nothing like a bath by candlelight, listening to Mozart or Bach or *The Archers* (a long-running BBC radio program about a rural farming village—terribly soothing) as the bubbles sink into your soul, and the Epsom salts remove whatever they remove, and tiny beads of perspiration form on your warmed skin.

MAKING A KINDNESS KIT

In the weeks leading up to the surgery, I started to collect all the items I would need in my house. Because, once I was on medical leave, I would be too sick to go out for a while.

I took a bento box and painted it and started to pop nice things into it, like tea lights and a yo-yo (nope, I've still not mastered it) and lovely rose-scented soap, lavender oil, and a notepad and pencils from the posh hotels I'd stayed in on business trips.

About halfway through, I realized what I'd done—I had made a kindness kit for myself. And for the first time since the diagnosis, I sat down on the sofa and wept.

Being kind to myself was a foreign concept.

If you can relate to that sentence, let's make a kindness kit for you. Here's how I made mine.

Because I would not be able to go out to the shops, I collected sweet objects to have around me that would allow me to get through sleepless nights, long days, and the bits in between. I also wanted everything to be beautiful, so I threw out boring soaps and bought little guest soaps with gorgeous scents. I bought a hand fan from a Chinese store that made me feel like a princess. Lavender sachets made tearful nights easier when slipped under the pillow. I knew I would write, so I collected pencils from glorious hotels and little notepads to have by the bed. Going to the post office would not be an option, so to stay in touch and say thank you for the flowers I received, I prestamped pretty postcards that friends could drop in the mailbox for me. The yo-yo might be frustrating. My friend Maria says it is. Try bubbles instead to make you smile.

THE MAGICAL NATURE OF TEA

Do you have a kettle and a milk pan? I have one of those French enamel milk pans, and it made the late-night hot-chocolate-and-tears sessions most soothing. How about lovely cups and saucers?

When I got sick, I started to notice how beautiful everyday household objects can be. And if there were some that I did not believe to be beautiful (yes, paraphrasing William Morris there), I got rid of them.

It's funny how sensitive we become when we're sick and tired and in need of some tea and sympathy. Even if you're not English, you might be surprised how lovely it is to make a pot of tea and sit quietly during the wee hours, sipping from an elegant bone china cup.

THE DELIGHTS OF DÉCOUPAGE

Back onto the subject of feelings for a moment. It was suggested to me, by others wiser and more experienced at looking after themselves, that I might want to express my anger and rage and frustration and sadness by doing art projects.

I blanched at this.

Seriously?

Crafts? Me?

But it was actually a brilliant suggestion (and now, of course, I'm obsessed with découpage and could talk to you about the different types of glazes for hours).

I had not made anything with my own hands for years. (I mean, who has time? Let alone the art supplies just hanging around.)

And I have no pretensions to having a deeply buried need to paint (although I love taking photographs—as I mentioned at the beginning, all the pictures in this book are mine).

But there's something childlike and joyful about getting messy and covered in glitter and glue.

So I did. I got covered in sparkly découpage Mod Podge glaze and stockpiled a stack of glossy magazines to cut up and ordered prints of my own photographs and some canvas boards, and it was SO MUCH FUN. I collaged away a great deal of my brooding depression. Try it! Pop some art supplies into your kindness kit—you know you want to. Some of mine became vision boards that created an image of my future life in Los Angeles (where I am writing this now!). Others were on themes of beauty (I have a particular love of 18th-century France—bring on the chandeliers!).

MOVIES ON THE LAPTOP

So you're taking the time for yourself to rest and nest and recover. Bravo. This is definitely when you can revisit all the movies and television programs that got you through your painful crush-laden and despair-driven teenage and college years. As well as catch up with those DVD box sets that your friends were raving about last year.

Line up the DVDs (or if, as my friend William says, you're Very Modern, those movies on demand) and snuggle into bed.

Sleeplessness (especially if you're in physical pain or discomfort for any reason) is a horrid by-product of being totally burned out. Movies make it all just about bearable.

On *teamgloria* I asked for people's lists of favorite foreign films and magical movies, and I received a ton of delicious suggestions.

The movies (and TV box sets) that got me through the midnight hour appear in the silver screen shopping list at the back of the book.

What would be your take-to-your-bed movies and TV box sets? Answers on a postcard, please (or, you know, the newfangled way, by leaving them in the comments at teamgloria.com).

I started with Doris Day, *Moonlighting*, and a few sensual foreign love stories—how about you? ;-)

PERFECT PLAYLISTS

Sometimes during my medical leave, I got so down I could barely stand myself.

And that's when the only thing that helped was music. I would listen to my iPod for hours, wondering when I'd get my life back (although, by that point, I had a sneaking suspicion I wasn't going to want what I used to have in the way of a life).

Now, I don't have a large music collection. But I know a lot of men, like my friend Ian, who do. In fact, most of my male friends are serious collectors who slice and dice their listening pleasure by decade, mood, or some other strange and wondrous cataloging method known only to them.

So I asked them to make playlists and burn CDs for me. This was magical. A lot of my male friends felt utterly powerless in the face of my illness, and they told me that working on a Sophia playlist gave them a sense of pride that they were helping. They really were—some of those music compilations are works of art.

I cannot recommend this highly enough for your sojourn at home—for however long it takes—ask your friends to make you playlists to while away the hours. Musical taste is so individual that I hesitated over whether or not to include a shopping list. But I've noted some tracks that I listened to over and over again that I hope you'll enjoy too.

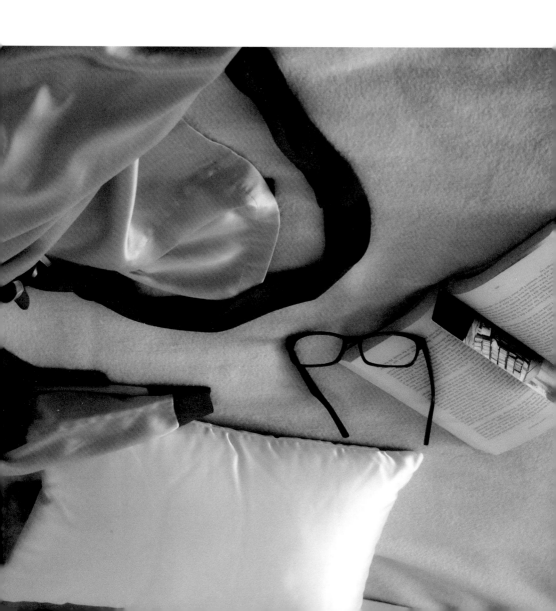

BOOKS AS COMPANIONS

Books have always played a huge part in my life. How about yours? They make the best companions, right? Well, maybe not the best. Well, sometimes. ;-)

I actually ran a small lending library out of my bedroom when I was nine (yes, I was horribly bossy at an early age and even, I blush to admit, charged late fees).

And book people are the best. I have a few people in my life who not only work in the publishing industry but are also published authors, like my friend Jacqueline, who sent piles of books, carefully chosen, for every hour and mood. There were books to uplift, books to be kind, books to invigorate, books to make one cry, and books to illustrate how to walk through painful stuff and find a light on the other side.

As I was on medical leave for a while, I asked three different friends a day to come visit—and read to me.

Oh! When was the last time someone read to you? Snuggling down on the sofa, wrapped in a soft pashmina and fluffy socks while someone opens a book and starts to read is so comforting. Particularly when it's Armistead Maupin's *Tales of the City*.

In fact, my friend William bought me the entire series as an audiobook, so Armistead himself could read to me during the many hours of sleeplessness. I posted about this on *teamgloria* and sent a thank you note to Armistead to tell him—and he wrote back (God, the best feeling in the world).

Would you do me the honor of sharing your books on teamgloria.com?

TIME TO REST NOW

So here you are. Ready for bed. For as long a time as you can steal from your daily life.

I hope you're not on medical leave. But if you are, just know that there will be a stretch of healing ahead and that you can get through it.

I did.

And there was something good that came out of my experience (you're reading it now). But I wouldn't want to go back to the beginning, to the diagnosis, or to the morning before the surgery, when Margot met me outside my house at 4:30 A.M. and I shook all the way to the hospital in the cab. Or to the bit where I was on the gurney with various medical professionals looking down at me before I counted back from ten. And especially not to the horrifying bit when I came round in the ICU, dripping with sweat, nurses removing the mask so I could try and breathe without the ventilator.

THE SCAR

I hesitated over sharing this picture with you.

But it's the truth. I have a scar.

And it took a long time to heal.

My friend Tina peered at my scar and said, "I rather like it." Followed by, "The pearls help." Which made me giggle and helped with the healing, too.

Gather up your pillows and a box of Kleenex, a novel, and some tea—it's time to rest.

It took a disaster of my own to see that many people are heading toward one themselves, if they don't stop now and take it easy. But if I hadn't gone through all that, I would not be writing this to you now. I would not have had the incredible experience of meeting many of you on teamgloria .com and hearing your stories.

It's now eighteen months since my surgery, and my life is transformed. I left my job because I decided it was time to go back to my original dream of making a living as a writer and photographer. I also wanted to move back to Los Angeles. And that's where I am. It was a long road to get back here and very hard to leave NYC and all the trappings that go with a lady executive's life. But I am so happy. My first one-woman photography show was in SoHo, in Manhattan, and I could not stop smiling through the opening night.

I am so excited to see what happens with this book that you are now reading. It feels like we're starting a movement of learning to slow down. There's nothing to be lost by stepping back and taking to your bed. Gather up beautiful items for your kindness kit and then sink back against those soft pillows and dream. It's time to rest, rejuvenate, and appreciate just how glorious life really is.

A FEW
Shopping Lists

*Take-to-Your-Bed **Kindness** Kit*

nice china **teacup** and saucer; **creams** for face, hands, and feet; tea lights for **candlelit baths**; essential oil burner; **crisp cotton pillowcases**; soft socks; soothing blue **brushed-cotton robe**; piles of clean white T-shirts; comfy **knickers**; bubble bath and oils and Epsom salts; **cashmere scarf** (I carried mine around like a blanket from room to room); lots of boxes of tissues (for tears and sniffles, and good with **lavender** oil drops to put over your eyes while napping); **tea—English breakfast,** afternoon Earl Grey, late-night herbal types; **art supplies**—canvas, paints, brushes, Mod Podge découpage glaze, stick-on **pearls,** lots of magazines, scissors, glue, sticky tape; lots of **playlist** CDs; **books-books-books**; movies that make you smile, movies that make you weep, **foreign films** that make you want to travel; lots of **notebooks** and pencils; candles for every mood (**rose** for healing, lavender for sleep-inducing—but blow them out before you do sleep!); fan (hand one from a Chinatown supply store and a **vintage** one for the bedroom to keep the air moving); telephone (call people from your **boudoir** to catch up); soft fruits like **peaches** and raspberries; **Greek yogurt** (soothing to the throat, kind to sore stomachs); **Italian mineral water** (to be served in **blue** glasses with ice and **lemon**).

Silver *Screen Therapy*

Pretty in Pink (swoony teen love), ***State and Main*** (Hollywood hipsters), ***Before Sunrise*** (and ***Before Sunset***—#sigh), the first two seasons of ***Moonlighting*** (don't you love their snappy dialogue and Maddie Hayes's silky satin '80s blouses?), ***Nurse Jackie*** (huge crush on Edie Falco), ***Cold Comfort Farm*** (witty, pretty, and terribly British and fun), ***Ferris Bueller's Day Off*** (exhilarating), ***The Fifth Element*** (Bruce Willis rocks; JPG's costumes are a dream; Chris Tucker is sublime), ***Friday Night*** (French—very sexy), ***The Love Letter*** (summer love in linens), ***Mostly Martha*** (German chef, melting love), ***Lover Come Back*** (Doris!), ***Moonstruck*** (Cher!), ***Desperately Seeking Susan*** (Madonna!), ***Switch*** (Ellen Barkin—clever genderness and office politics turned on its head), ***Victor Victoria*** ("How long have you been a homosexual?" "How long have you been a soprano?"), ***A Christmas Tale*** (Deneuve as a matriarch, Mathieu Almaric as the unruly offspring), ***Studio 60 on the Sunset Strip*** (brilliance), the **Thin Man** series (box set—Nick and Nora—Manhattan madness in monochrome '30s decors—what's not to love?), ***The Breakfast Club*** (remember feeling that powerless and rebellious? Yup, me too), ***St. Elmo's Fire*** (oh, wow, Domi having a meltdown with the silk drapes billowing and the boys on the fire escape and Andrew McCarthy flicking ash into the wok), ***Lipstick Jungle*** (so on the money—the shoes, the meetings-as-duels-at-dawn), *The Thomas Crown Affair* (all the money in the world can't buy illicit thrills), *Beloved* (Paul Schneider's best role ever), *Elizabethtown* (60B!), *Withnail and I* ("I think an evening at the Crow"—William and I used this line constantly in Cornwall on holiday), and, of course, *When Harry Met Sally* (RIP, Nora Ephron). Oh, yes, and box sets of *The Golden Girls* (Rose's stories, Blanche's caftans, and Dorothy's deliciously deep drawl).

Magical **Music**

"A Whiter Shade of Pale," **Procol Harum** (opening shots to *Withnail and I*); "All of Me," **Frank Sinatra** (Lily and Steve dancing); "Don't Play That Song," **Aretha Franklin**; "Bonamana," **Super Junior** (delicious K-pop); "Mi Princesa," **David Bisbal** (Latin yearnings—from Latin America, not *amo, amas, amat* ;-)); "Recuerdame," **La Quinta Estacion** (more Latino passion); "Jin Chi," **Faye Wong** (plaintive Chinese ballad); "Pain Love," **Joey Yung** (another plaintive Chinese song but with a rousing build on lead guitar); "I Want You to Want Me," **Cheap Trick**; "Sunday Morning," **Velvet Underground**; "London," **The Smiths**; "Big Black Smoke," **The Kinks**; "Dance Me to the End of Love," **Leonard Cohen**; "One Fine Day," **Natalie Merchant**; "La Soledad," **Pink Martini**; "More Than This," **Roxy Music**; "Slave to Love," **Bryan Ferry**; "Wild Hearted Woman," **All About Eve**; "This Year's Kisses," **Nina Simone**; "Summer Wine," **The Corrs**; "Danny's All-Star Joint," **Rickie Lee Jones**; "Xanadu," **Olivia Newton-John** (hey, you had roller skates and a shiny spandex catsuit back in the day, right?); "Black on Black," **Dalbello**; "Kids," **Robbie Williams** (with **Kylie**); "All the Lovers," **Kylie Minogue**; "Alphabet St.," **Prince**; "All Along the Watchtower," **Jimi Hendrix**; "Song to the Siren,"

This Mortal Coil; "The Host of Seraphim," **Dead Can Dance** (yup, had a thing about goths at one point ;-)); "Girls Just Want to Have Fun," **Cyndi Lauper** (saw her standing on the corner of Broadway and 54th in 2007—omg—luminous); "What'll I Do," **Chet Baker**; "'S Wonderful," **Diana Krall**; "Rock You Like a Hurricane," **Scorpions**; "Life in Tokyo," **Japan**; "Forbidden Colours," **David Sylvian**; "Yes," **McAlmont and Butler**; "Tainted Love," **Soft Cell**; "Modern Love," **David Bowie**.

Books as *Companions*

Country Notes in Wartime, **Vita Sackville-West**; *The Water Beetle*, **Nancy Mitford** (basically anything and everything by N. Mitford—she wrote the palest pink-fondant-iced gems of literature—delicious); *Pleasures and Landscapes*, **Sybille Bedford** (ditto: everything Sybille ever wrote is a sumptuous sensual treat); *Paris Was Yesterday*, **Janet "Genet" Flanner**; *Future Indefinite*, **Noel Coward** (the diaries are wonderful too, and the plays sublime, particularly *Design for Living*); *The Most of P. G. Wodehouse* (I reread this anthology every winter—everything I learned about being Natania's aunt I got from reading Plum Wodehouse); *We Tell Ourselves Stories in Order to Live*, **Joan Didion** (incredible prose and intense observation of others and of self and of being there in the '60s and what it means to be from California); *The Fran Lebowitz Reader* (my dream dinner companion—the line "He is audibly tan" still has me in pieces . . . I sit at the Waverly Inn, hoping she'll drop by); *Jane Trahey on Women and Power* (this is a gem from the '70s on how to get ahead in advertising and life by one of the first women to put up her own Madison Avenue shingle); *Exhumations*, **Christopher Isherwood** (his essay on Santa Monica is my favorite); I used to read from *The Complete Works of*

Shakespeare on my morning commute to the office on the 1 subway train from SoHo to Columbus Circle (it's on my Kindle app on the iPod and BlackBerry—I don't carry a physical copy around with me ;-)); *Comfort Me with Apples*, **Ruth Reichl**; *Slow Love*, **Dominique Browning**; *The Art of Doing Nothing*, **Veronique Vienne**; and everything **Joan Juliet Buck** has ever written on desire and moving to Santa Fe, living in Italy and riding around in the back of a Fiat 500, and eating a chili pepper in an open-top car, but most especially her ghost story from when she was editor in chief at Paris *Vogue*.

your notes to share on *teamgloria*

I'd love to hear from you. Would you drop by teamgloria.com and stay awhile and tell me how you're doing? Isn't that the most delicious thing about the Internet? We can keep talking, wherever we are. Since I started my blog, I've met wonderful people who happened to drop by. Visitors to the site appear from all over the world—I have new friends in Arles (France), Whitstable (England), Christchurch (New Zealand), and lots in Berlin—and some of them I have even met in real life too.

Go on, write to us. Please.

who is *teamgloria?*

Sophia Stuart is a writer, photographer, and award-winning digital strategist/creative director with over 17 years of experience in building digital products within the USA & international (Asia/Europe) publishing and Hollywood movie industries. She has created digital products for New Line Cinema (*Take the Lead* motion capture/online game) and 20th Century Fox (*The Devil Wears Prada* website/online game/publication). Voted one of the "Top 21 Social Media Superstars" by Min Online in 2009, she won a Webby Award for Cosmo Mobile USA (2008) and an MVA for Cosmo International Digital Strategy (2010) while at Hearst as head of mobile (USA) and then head of digital (International) with responsibility for the digital vision/strategy for 300 international brands including *Cosmo*, *Harper's BAZAAR*, and *Esquire* in countries including China, India, Hong Kong, Italy, France, and South Africa.

She consults for Sony TV/Cosine Three, is on the Advisory Board for fashion start-up Buy My Closet, and has personal clients in Hollywood for whom she manages social media strategy and more. She writes a weekly column for Los Angeles, I'm Yours, and blogs at teamgloria.com. Her business site is sophiastuart.com.

Hay House Titles of Related Interest

YOU CAN HEAL YOUR LIFE, the movie, starring Louise L. Hay & Friends
(available as a 1-DVD program and an expanded 2-DVD set)
Watch the trailer at: www.LouiseHayMovie.com

THE SHIFT, the movie,
starring Dr. Wayne W. Dyer
(available as a 1-DVD program and an expanded 2-DVD set)
Watch the trailer at: www.DyerMovie.com

* * *

THE ART OF EXTREME SELF-CARE: Transform Your Life One Month at a Time,
by Cheryl Richardson

BE HAPPY: Release the Power of Happiness in YOU,
by Robert Holden, Ph.D.

INTEGRATIVE WELLNESS RULES: A Simple Guide to Healthy Living,
by Dr. Jim Nicolai

LIGHT THE FLAME: 365 Days of Prayer,
by Andrew Harvey

All of the above are available at your local bookstore,
or may be ordered by contacting Hay House (see next page).

* * *

We hope you enjoyed this Hay House book. If you'd like to receive our
online catalog featuring additional information on Hay House books and products,
or if you'd like to find out more about the Hay Foundation, please contact:

Hay House, Inc., P.O. Box 5100, Carlsbad, CA 92018-5100
(760) 431-7695 or (800) 654-5126
(760) 431-6948 (fax) or (800) 650-5115 (fax)
www.hayhouse.com® • www.hayfoundation.org

* * *

Published and distributed in Australia by: Hay House Australia Pty. Ltd., 18/36 Ralph
St., Alexandria NSW 2015 • *Phone:* 612-9669-4299 • *Fax:* 612-9669-4144
www.hayhouse.com.au

Published and distributed in the United Kingdom by: Hay House UK, Ltd., Astley
House, 33 Notting Hill Gate, London W11 3JQ • *Phone:* 44-20-3675-2450
Fax: 44-20-3675-2451 • www.hayhouse.co.uk

Published and distributed in the Republic of South Africa by: Hay House SA (Pty),
Ltd., P.O. Box 990, Witkoppen 2068 • *Phone/Fax:* 27-11-467-8904 • www.hayhouse.co.za

Published in India by: Hay House Publishers India, Muskaan Complex,
Plot No. 3, B-2, Vasant Kunj, New Delhi 110 070 • *Phone:* 91-11-4176-1620
Fax: 91-11-4176-1630 • www.hayhouse.co.in

Distributed in Canada by: Raincoast Books, 2440 Viking Way, Richmond, B.C.
V6V 1N2 • *Phone:* 1-800-663-5714 • *Fax:* 1-800-565-3770 • www.raincoast.com

* * *

Take Your Soul on a Vacation

Visit www.HealYourLife.com® to regroup, recharge, and
reconnect with your own magnificence.
Featuring blogs, mind-body-spirit news, and
life-changing wisdom from Louise Hay and friends.

Visit www.HealYourLife.com today!

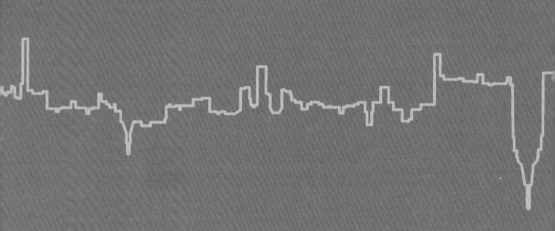